THE ARRANGEMENT OF SPACE

THE ARRANGEMENT OF SPACE

Martha Collins

PEREGRINE SMITH BOOKS

SALT LAKE CITY

First edition
95 94 93 92 91 5 4 3 2 1

Published by Gibbs Smith, Publisher, Peregrine Smith Books, P.O. Box 667, Layton, Utah 84041 (801) 544-9800

Design by Kathleen Timmerman

Cover photograph, *Untitled*, 1987 by Zeke Berman

Printed and bound in the United States of America

Library of Congress Cataloging-in-Publication Data

Collins, Martha,
The arrangement of space / Martha Collins.
p. cm.—(The Peregrine Smith poetry series)
ISBN 0-87905-390-9 : $9.95
I. Title. II. Series.
PS3553.04752A87 1991 91-8055
811'.54—dc20 CIP

Contents

Women in American Literature: An Introduction

for F. A. Austin

WOMEN IN AMERICAN LITERATURE: AN INTRODUCTION

1.

This is the story some of us tell, the one
about the woman in white, the way she dances
with everyone, the way she lights a thin
cigarette and everyone laughs except the child.
The way she is ready for anything, the way
the roses appear in her hair.

                                        Here she is gray,
with light in her eyes, and the story begins at the edge
of the woods, at the edge of town, in a small house.
When we come, she opens the door and we think
She is thinking of us, as we eye the white streaks
in her hair, but she was never a child.

As the story begins she is hemming a sleeve, a dark
sleeve with a silk-bound hem, and I am turning
a pearl in my fingers, the sea, the long way home
to the woman who cuts and loops and binds, but now
it is time we got in the car.

                                        'Julie,' you say,
and I say 'Ben,' shaping the sound, holding the *n*
for the first time, forgetting Sarah and Danny,
brother and sister, friend and friend, who sit
in the back seat of your long black car. Danny
is reading Indian poems; Sarah is thinking
of being a nun; you're a country lawyer
who raises goats.

                              'Heroes,' you say.
'Sheroes,' I say, 'in my story, she
rose.' 'No,' you smile, 'he rose.'
Rose. Red. Blue. *And violates?*

2.

We're deep in the hills, in the noon sun, when we come
to the town where I leave you alone, I need to see
how far she saw on her own. Because if I
can find her here, not in the center, its tall
dark steeples, not even the seven doors of the house,
but all around, where her business lay, on the edge,
the measureless rim of the circle that turns both ways
at once—

'No,' I say, when you start from the car,
'this is for me,' and Sarah takes my hand
and we walk through the gate to the white front door.

But she's not here, the woman in white, only
a dress, and a paisley shawl, and the Civil War blanket
she used in the garden, though there is something whole
and done. 'The undivided self,' says Sarah;
'the nuns know.' 'But all alone, and giving up—?'
'She got herself. She put on her body to write.'

We walk in the garden, among the grass, where all
the flowers are growing up, and the petals glow,
a little rose, stretching, opening, full.

'Julie, they want less of us, they want
us half, when we need whole.'

And opposition's
complement is opposition still.

3.

At the edge of the next state she waits in a house
for something to do. Two white doors on two
red slabs, a double house that inside comes
together. She lifts her head, rises, stands,
framed in a doorway dimly lit with light
from the green-shaded lamps on the library table.
She has been trying to read, she says, and I start
to speak, I'm alone this time—

But then you're there
and we're off again, in the back seat, your hand
is moving and Danny is driving and Sarah
is sleeping and I am trying to read a book
but your hand

and now she remembered the story she'd told,
he was Gil, the taker of hostages, fish, but she hadn't
remembered that book, that snake in the garden

and farther along a green-hilled town, I know
a bridge, a woman said—

'Let the women
go,' you say, 'Daddy's here,' and your hand
is moving— 'But she knew what to do. She helped
me see.' A swinging bridge across a gorge.
The hills outside. The clouds like smoke. The two-
part house, and the lady there: she knew too,
and what she did was think. But now I am thinking
of what you are doing. Your hand inside. The hills
like smoke. Trying to think— Your hand like clouds—
The hills inside— Sarah and Danny— 'Oh!'

4.

'Look at that!' Danny cries. I wake
up slow, rub my eyes; Sarah has a hand
on Danny's shoulder. Then I see the hills
like thickened thighs, and there, through darkness, trees,
through Danny's eyes, in mist, the feathered heads,
the carried bows.

                                        Sarah points, 'And that,'
she says, and there, ahead, the smaller forms,
framed in leaves, fresh and curled and spotless
under siege. One is dark, hair
and eye and skin, she has a body, leads
the way. The other's blonde and blue and slight,
she folds her lily hands.

                                                    'Fair she marries, dark
she dies,' I say, and Danny: 'White man, red.'
'Except,' you say, raising your head from my lap,
'for our man the hero.'

                                                    And there he is, tall
as trees, alone and heading west
like us, loving his dog and his accurate gun,
married to woods, to rushing streams, to winds
that ripple the boughs of the trees,

                                                                    and now I'm a child
and the woman is fixing our dinner and there he is,
from out of the radio past, he sits alone
at the edge of a cliff, chin in his hand, but at last
he stands, guns on his hips, in his white hat

and black mask, and says: 'No! Love
is not for me';

and that's when, twelve years old,
I say, *'I* wouldn't, if it weren't for sex,'
and she, unshocked, spoon in her hand, says 'Neither
would anyone else.'

Then I'm sadder still,
as if he'd killed, as if she'd died for love,
in the tall pines where I walk with her, around
until we meet ourselves, armed with trowels,
in the bright ferns, my lady of the lake.

5.

This is my father's kind of place, clean
and large and slightly dark, *lots of cars, it must*
be good, my father's words,

but the service
is slow and the fat steaks aren't fat enough
and the water is cloudy and everyone's edgy and then
you beckon, your single finger, the tall black waiter,
and 'Boy,' you say and 'Boy!' you say and drop
a single dime on the white-covered table.

Danny's off and Sarah plans, but I
will try to understand, and when you start
to cry I almost stay. Then Sarah frowns,

takes my hand and says, 'Remember those hills,
that swinging bridge?'

                                        We double back and find
the bridge and the rain begins and we find a cave
and wait for the storm that doesn't come,
the only sound's the long white rush of water
into the gorge. Then at last we sway
across, in the green air, in the green rain,
and I am forgetting everything, lost
in green, when Sarah says, 'It's us, it's ours
to bridge—'

                              And the fingers that are these lakes
are long, they beckon and bend, the road curves
close to the water, we walk and walk and walk
and turn into town,

                                        where we ask for the woman who knew,
who said, who lived here, married, had a friend,
and close to the river we find the house where she rose
one day from her round table, to call to her boys
in the cherry trees, to please come down, to not
throw stones, and began to think of a way to use her tongue:

Susan! Susan! Susan! You must manage
to spend a week with me   A terrible scourging
when last at my father's   Henry sides with my friends
They are not willing that I should write
Sometimes, Susan, I struggle in deep waters

6.

Now we're headed west again, Sarah
and I on a Greyhound bus, pretending we're running
away from home, we'll take new names and rent
small rooms, I'll get a job in a roadside diner
that's open all night for ham and eggs.

In fact
we're circling a city we know, and then it's motels,
motels, motels, with honeymoon specials and breakfasts
and pools, and we stop at a place that looks and sounds
like everywhere else as much as itself:
Africans, Indians, Spanish, French, it seems
a dream of another time, except for the clothes,
the cameras, the money. Why do they come to this place?

Then we see the first white rush, like thick
white hair, and then we're there, where whiteness falls
in one deep curve, a whiteness circling whiteness,
arced by a rainbow, colors thick as things
you could touch, you could hold, and I think of a hunter
coming upon it, the first to see: 'Now
I could pray,' I whisper to Sarah, who touches my arm
and says, 'I'll tell you a secret.'

But there's a hand
on my other arm, and there you are, with Danny
behind you, you've got a little black kid beside you,
you're smiling and saying, 'Hi there! Need a ride?'
The kid smiles; he's got a balloon. 'Somebody needs
a mother,' you say. I frown and you say, 'A sister
then.' I turn to Sarah and then you say,
'Julie, Jewels, I'm sorry. I made a mistake.'

You lift the kid in your arms, the red balloon
wavers, then rises straight, and I see how the spray
has moistened your different skins. 'I'll take him back
to his mother,' you say; 'then we'll be on our way.'

7.

This is someone else's land, we've crossed
the river, the border, the line, the money is strange,
the ads, the signs, though the trees are apple and peach
in rows, and the fields are familiar vineyards, thick
with leaves, before the grapes.

'*Gonna live off the fat
of the land,*' you say, 'who said that?' I turn
my eyes, your hand's on the wheel. 'My father, I think.'
The wind's in your hair. '*Grapes of Wrath.* Lennie
said that.' 'Lennie's *Mice and Men.* He plays
with the mice.'

But you're right, this country looks like that,
California, the place we're going, the sun
has already set on that ocean, it's crossed the fields
of artichokes with mustard growing between
the rows, it's set on the edge of that land that is
our own, our last frontier.

'You sure?' you say,
and I've lost the thread, I'm already there, but then
I remember, I hesitate, and 'Yes,' I say,
and you say, 'Thank you, Teacher. Anytime.'

Anytime? That's my line, but that's
the way you manage words, you make them make
us notice you, different from Sarah and Danny
and me, richer, older, known in the world—

*Why had she done this crazy thing? Because
the well was dry, she had no work to do.
Because her garden had not come up,
because there was something she had to learn.
Because, she thought, he was different: it might be him.*

A Book of Days

for Sharon Dunn

1

In the story, she gives him everything,
that he should be nothing
without her, who has too much.

An old story.

In mine she runs, wrapped in a pink blanket.

    Made myself naked, unfastened myself
    from myself like leaves but myself hangs on,
    mittens dancing below my hands—

Bricks turn unfamiliar, pink, windows gape
like missing teeth, the blank face
of the sky is turning away—

Caught in a branch of that plot again,
the dark lines the light draws—

            And where shall I go to find her?

2

Veterans Day

The game is Kill the King, he said.
A little Freud he'd read somewhere.
Things about women, too.

But when he was king he did nothing,
except say No, except say Do,
and then, early one morning, he said Die.

Trenches I can imagine.
Rats, vermin, water and mud. The standing
there, the waiting, the Over the Top.

Because something has to move.
The field itself, if nothing else.

Listen: *I* was the battlefield.
Mine, he said. Me, he said,
swaying in his underwear, little boy
on a bare floor, and told me about his mother,
popping up and up and up in an old dream.

Machine guns you could hold in your hands,
and tanks, those armored beasts, and planes,
and bombs in the air, and submarines—

It used to be the armistice.
Now we remember the ones who fought.

Understand: I was trying to win myself.

3

'After nine years,' you said last night,
'even Achilles stopped being angry.'
Then you smiled and spoke of yourself
as if you were someone you cared about.

I'd never seen you like that before.
You'd never seen me like this—

> *Running down the street that night*
> *in a blanket, seeing a blurred world,*
> *lights like yellow chrysanthemums,*
> *she thought of men with bows and arrows,*
> *shooting tiny birds. She thought of women*
> *grinding corn. She saw her hair,*
> *long again, in braids.*

It wasn't much: a man and a woman
going to dinner, deciding what dishes to share,
doing something they'd done before.

But today the people sit on the grass,
they walk on the walks with their books and bags,
they play in the leaves with their children.

Over and over and over, I thought,
this morning, passing the sycamores.
Over meaning *Again,* and *Never again,* and *I have spoken.*

4

Ice this morning, cracked, by the curb,
cellophane, glass. Frost on the bricks.
The playground closed for the season.

Last night, I think, and across the street
a carpenter tap tap taps new boards to a house.

Once a child played in this place. He crawled
through the space of that upright tire—

Last night I saw you a row ahead
and raised my arm to reach
my hand to your shoulder and stopped,
frozen, mid-air, as if
on film, and as quickly drew my hand
back toward my body.

My ungloved hand begins to ache.
My other rattles the keys in my pocket.

The ground is littered with seeds from an ash,
exclamations without a point—

This is my hand on your shoulder.
This is the other side, the space
that's given and taken at once.

Space to be arranged like chairs,
easy chairs in front of a fire.

Space that's room like the separate rooms
where we live and open our books, our mouths
to someone who's always someone else
on the other side of the space, the air we breathe.

5

The screen grids, grays a little the dappled sky.

The blue places between
the clouds:

        to tongue them into meaning
        morning light—

Last month, the girl who lives
most well in her own mind
was first to see the pigeons on the cornice.
A white one, she cried, and I thought Dove.

That was before the troubled time.

The fire escape is mostly space.

Things are written under things.

Life's below, where snow patches grass.

I have held on.

6

Emily Dickinson, 1830-1886

Deep in the hills, in the noon sun,
through the white gate, through the white front door,
up the stairs to the room, and the white dress—

Up the stairs, to the cupola,
where the turning world—the trees, the hills,
the hills beyond circumference—returned.

Is this what body comes to, then,
after the dinners, the talk, the wine,
hello, goodbye, is this the way,
most I, most who I am?

He was perfect muse, the god who was
and was not there. She had no mother,
she said, her mother was awe.

But awe was also muse, was house,
was hills, beyond the hills—

Mother, wife, the earth at last.
For us it goes the other way:

the deep green cave, the flesh
of love, the wings
of the white election—

7

On the plane the babies are starting to sing,
wedding themselves to the new world.

Outside, the ground is soft
and white, the walls are the blue
that can't get through, we're held
by sheer air.

            A blue world, the babies
            have not forgotten,

while I have just
remembered again, no one holding
me up or down, no strings

attached, no harness

        to no balloon, no plodding thing.

8

Christmas Afternoon

They've drained the old pond, they're digging it deeper.
Two derricks face each other across the mud,
stumps, rubble, brush,
an oval of water, wrinkled like skin,
that yesterday was rain.

All right. I cried last night when the choir sang
and almost cried when the brass band played
in the almost April weather of late December.

This morning not the want, but the wanting not.

Across the street, wind chimes chime.

On the other bank three small trees
are growing together: an I, a Y, an intricate shape,
a woman leaning into the wind,
arms raised, breasts, straining against
the limbs of the others, who hold her there.

Everyone alive in the world is very nearly the same age.

I am still the baby in that house.

9

People with two dogs run in the yard with their two dogs.

When I started to run, I ran around
a three-mile pond, meeting, sometimes, the priest
before morning mass, or the old woman who looked contempt
at my blue shoes:
                    'In my time,' she said once,
'women got their exercise at home.'

Last night in the film the man became
the woman and then the man for the woman he loved:
for her, the whole old story at once,
the best parts of its plots.

Between the patterns
the terriers make,
                    the upright creature,
covered in bright cloth, starts
and stops and starts and stops and claps her hands.

10

Epiphany

At last, snow, flocked
like cotton, clusters, blossoms, stuff
comes down—

so little wind you feel the pull,
as of apples, the weight of body
toward the knees—

Hark! the Herald Angels Sing, bells
announce, trumpets, wings, everything
lifted, raised—

Down below, the grass is green, walks
are wet, people are carrying gloves
and bright umbrellas—

Not the flash, the blinding light, tongues,
as of fire, but the coming to see,
on the edge of a warm winter
like this,

this shortened but lengthening day—

Coming to see, one feels less seen,
less haloed, held, more fallen
like snow turned rain
to earth to peace to mercy
to all that rages that aches that cries
that whimpers that turns that catches
its breath that breathes—

11

Late afternoon, the eight-chimneyed building
across the yard, clock on its gable,
lights up, as if with fire, in every window.
An excess: the sky is still light,
or almost light, and something about
that light, the white trim, the slate
gray roof, the air itself, the lucent sky,
seems single, almost a surface you could polish.

I have never felt empty.
Once, when I was a child,
I felt too full, and sometimes at night.

Now this light, this stranger light,
so different from everything else
it seems the same—

Walking around the world this way,
as if a world were being made—

Nothing slips through the net, falls from the basket.
The earth, inside its porous skin, is whole.

12

Like two sides of a leaf,
not this brown, but a still-green leaf,
are not-snow and snow
in a warm winter.

On the other side of a new way
of seeing is something old:
a shadow tree, an under-
flow,
        bands of being run
together, stretching,
bending, slack.

In the rain forest, the golden frog
rides the darker, twice-as-large
not-gold female frog.
                                        They work
together, outside themselves,
eggs laid over a pool, or over a leaf
that's over a pool.

Something else is on top now.
The old is merely clinging, like the dust
that's skin, or pollen,
to the belly.

13

A man in a little white truck
with red wheels and a black scoop
is clearing the walks.
                                    Beep beep he comes
to a halt, lifts, then lowers the scoop
with a lilt, like a dancer's arm.

The snow comes down.
It crosses itself, it rises
in little leaps.

This morning I felt a trouble start
to rise, light as a layer
of lace—
          then fall
with the weight of snow that falls
from the roof, like bundled cargo.

Then rise, then start to rise again.

Now it rests
like the light cover in which
the heart, warm, in a safe place, lies
and goes, little machine, about its work.

14

On a train I rarely take, I look up,
expecting green.
                    Of course it's gray, brown, white
where the light of early morning lines the trees:

I'm still in summer grass, that strange
green lake, in last night's dream.

People are getting hungrier,
people who've never taken vacations,
whose kids never went to camp,
who were hungry before.

Things have always been this way won't do.

I am hungry too won't do.

The honeycomb, the mole-rats,
the gibbons singing at dawn won't do.

We are all kin in this world,
who can think at dawn of other dawns,
who can dream of other dreams—

who can think of ending everything,
as if Won't were another, greener side of Won't do—

15

Red eye, red foot: the pigeons are finding
the roofs again, the fire escape, the cat
will be glad, or at least respond
to the flutter and flap on the other side
of the glass.

An icicle falls, not
on its point, but its side.

Beads of water cling to limbs, like buds
in the wrong place.

Leaves may come out
in the wrong place: they may have to turn,
like faces, to find the light.

In the store this morning, iris for sale.
Next door in the restaurant, fading poinsettias.

Rain, rain all day,
pocking the snow.

The single eye of the pigeon's the eye,
in the dream, of a cheap stuffed toy.

16

Last night I woke with a great fright,
too huge to come from a thing
so small, so crawling:

a whitish thing, but I thought of the ants
enslaving their prey, the smaller ants,
then letting themselves be fed, nested, moved
in the jaws of their slaves.

I let it grow, I tell you I made
that something grow, until its brittle legs
were long as bones, stripped, smooth,
almost ivory, firm, flesh
held to my face, my open mouth—

I loved her.

And then I let go.

17

This is one of those days of days,
one the others were waiting for.

It comes wearing nothing more stunning
than rain, a gray sky without silver
or pearl, rather like smoke, with even
a little yellow, a trace of bruise.

It's inside, the lining of sky,
the dream where the colors
re-enter the birds, the earth,
a place as ornately green as a gold
thing's gold, with birds in cages
so lightly barred they can fly
in and out, and grass so fine it's air,
and sky so royally blue it's a house,
the walls of an old Roman house, turned in-
side out, a dream so lovely I wake
myself up to see—

                    This is the day
the world of dream re-enters the world
where I live:
              a beech as barely gray
as the day, its long thin buds still wet
from the rain,
               a tree in the yard of a house
where I'm going, an open house where there are
no bars,
         a brilliantly opened and entered
                    and living space.

18

The sign taped to the telephone pole
says FOUND *something something* CAT
something something CALL—

It's still raining.

Cats and dogs, they'd say, and I'd see the air
slashed with the falling of the bodies.

Found again, as if for the first time.

That was this afternoon. Now I wake
so inside out I turn on the light
to turn it off to sleep—

It keeps on raining.
It keeps on raining rain.

19

The facade of the building across the yard
has forty windows, a calendar page
for Lent, with measured days—

In Guatemala, they cut out the tongues,
they cut the soles of the feet in pieces,
they burned the bodies in living piles.

In Europe, a young man killed
the woman he loved, he cut, he cooked,
he ate her tongue, her nose, her lips.

This is not inhuman.
This is not nature, discarding.

Someone I know has a sign on his desk,

* You can do no wrong *

If this isn't wrong, it's still not right.

Here is my building, here are my windows,
here are my days, my prayers, my penance,
my breath, my unburned sins, my undone loves.

20

Once, running for life, having nothing
to prove myself myself, I heard a steel door
slam shut and felt, on the narrow cot
beside the seatless toilet, safe.

At night, at home, when I look down
from my window, squares of light
pattern the blackness.

Lights go on and off all night,

and far away, in another state,
a man arrives at a city jail and claims
the frightened woman he calls *Mine.*

And what if an old and powerful man
in the threatened years of this century
should wish the whole world
to die with him, wife for his pyre?

21

The sycamores down by the river lean
toward the river.

In Hiroshima, the skull's mouth
opened for water; meat
walked on bones.

Not even the eye,
                                        the eye that strips
the bark from the bone-white trees,

is clean.

22

In the rain, the bark of the plane trees shines
in the colors, the shapes of camouflage:
trees looking like men looking like trees.

When the sun shines, the trees shade
the grass a darker green, the thick veins
of giant leaves, a giant's hands—

Terrain with deep cracks, that old puzzle—

In California, it rained on the queen
and the president, it rained on the good
and the bad, it rained on me.

In the jungle, it rained, it has rained,
it rains on bodies fallen
like leaves, on bodies that walk—

In the rain, the shadows disappear.

In a larger rain, things are lost.

In the largest rains, borders emerge—

A puzzle coming apart, becoming the world.

23

Easter Morning

Light! Light! The white inside
the church, the mouths of the lilies open
in every direction, the paned
white sky outside—

Inside, bits
of prayer: it is finished,
that painful time.

Finished for now, though the war dead die
as the war dead died, and we are not poor
in our hearts as the poor are poor.

This is what the angel said:

Not here, in this empty place,
but there, on the road to the place
you are going,
the place we are going
to now, through the clear rain.

24

Waiting, one feels time
the way one speaks of a tree,
meaning not, as here in this yard,
this beech, the dark marks of lovers
still on the skin, the ovals where limbs
were cut—
                    meaning rather the loss we hide
by counting up:

                         Up, the way the tree grows,
or the way we speak of a mountain,
forgetting the roots, the other side—

Tree as in family tree, or tree
as dreamed, as if in a place
like this—

                    Time like a mountain, an island
on land, the tree,
                              a ripened fruit as large
as the hand that holds the yellow half,
or the other hand, that scoops
the fat black seeds.

25

Pentecost

The sun gone for a moment, air
intrudes itself, a cool presence, bodies
stir on the warm grass—

The word gone, the red letters
of speech—lips held open, tongue held still,
nothing but vowels, oh, ooh, the ah
of pain, the uh of hurt, the hhh of almost
nothing left, the hush of nothing except
the slightest breath—

                                        the word gone, spirit
came, it filled, mouth to mouth,
the whole house.

                                    Then fire, a dazzle
of tongues, doing things over, things
that were done—

                                    the first breath breathed
        into something, then everyone
                talking at once—

A cloud slips from the shoulder
of the sun, the sun falls on the bodies stripped
again, the bodies houses filled with flesh—

For a moment, the house was nothing
but mouth, the tongue
of the body the tongue of the holiest ghost
of the word that was, that was to be—

26

As if the windows
were open air.
As if
the ground were nothing.

The old dream, the old wish,
but this time the wings
are my own open arms,
as if I had come to be
in the way of the birds, the little feet
lengthened and feathered, not as if
I were carrying something strange,
a burden grown from the bones
of my upright back.

As if
I were the very first
of my kind.

27

Beautiful is what she was.

Cut-glass bowls on her dressing table, mirror
above, hers
                    (his was long, framed
by the bedroom door).

The book's cover shuts
on its flyleaf, her
name touches his.

. . . in Paris,

now, drawing a cigarette
from the chalk-blue pack, pointing my elbows
into the white cloth, watching

her there, touching herself, pearl
after pearl after pearl against
her skin, making sure.

28

A simple plot:
just the cabbages,
                                        not the path
of the rabbit among them, not
the carrots, the rampant squash—

How much of what we have is useless:
                                                                        hair,
cells, bits of skin, remnants of what
we can't remember, love
of what never was—

At night, when the story's over, a light goes out.

29

The roses are washed out, the iris brown

like thin paper pressed between the folds
of a wedding dress, the bride
has gone, her child has gone, and she

knows something we don't know, the way
the body rends itself, is more
than one—she's known
for years, they won't let her forget.

Someone has turned the fountain off, the pool
is still, is almost still, it shifts
like an eye pretending not to shift, the breast looks

like an eye but it cannot see, only

the eye can see.

A sparrow drinks from the rim
of the pool, a bee disturbs its surface.

Nothing's whole.

30

Heavy the leaves, burdens,
little animals in the wind, paws, mouths.

To strip her down, take off
the green dress, the red shoes
under the soles of her feet, to open
her closed her nymph
her mermaid legs—

Is the sea open
or closed space?

The blue sea, the green sea,

the brown river we swam, suits
in our hands, the current
we rode—

Victim, I heard.

I felt the seal,
the openings closed.

Can this be power, this *open*?

Six Suites

for Barbara Johnson

WIND CHILL

1.

The snow blowing across the road,
chasing itself, the sun
midday, the cat's-eyes
of the oncoming cars, the car filling
with organ music as flesh is filled
with flesh, strange that anything opens at all—

2.

On a mountain one summer, the un-
cut grass, the monks hid their hands
beneath their robes, their voices waited
behind their tongues, the grass
bent down and then
stood up as if to speak.

3.

The snow blew into the little plane, the snow
glowed like lights in the light, the cold
touched our faces, fists, our hands
found each other, hand
over hand over body, body letting go.

4.

Smell of apples, mug of hot
rum, windows white, a child came out
where love went in, it was warm
in that house.

5.

The boy on the plane, his left hand
on my right breast, his right
under my skirt as the snow
blew in my life my life and then I will die.

6.

Open, as if the sun were a hole
in the gray sky, waiting for something to hold
in itself, the wind unlike the world
as a thing could be, the cold, the swell
of the organ, the chords, the rush
of snow blowing like God across the road.

INSIDE

1.

This time she called across the room while the rain
was turning to snow, the snow they both
desired, wind
in the thin trees.

Morning come, would the edge
be gone, lost
in the verbless snow?

2.

Inside, she was under someone, child

under the dining room table,
hugging its thick legs.

3.

And what if she couldn't get out
of there, what if the door closed
on her facing out the way
a window faces out
on her—

4.

She touched her over
her under between.

She called her by her name.

5.

That night, asleep, she wrapped him up
and sent him out.

When the package arrived, she let it in.

It thumped across the room.

6.

Inside, the light came on, sun
through the shadeless panes.

The stream clung to the low brush, froze
white, draped in that light.

She moved inside, as a woman moves into a room.

HAIR

1.

He sat on the stool waiting
for me. I kept

the appointment, his fingers quick
in my hair.

2.

Less, I said, meaning More.

3.

Always an edge, the scissors
meet, close, do not
cross, they open

and nothing's been lost that shouldn't
have been but what if they went

too far not to mention the point.

4.

Now I am thinking
of her, our legs cross
like scissors but do not cut we are each

of us singular, plural as love, love.

5.

I waited for him as long as I could.

The only way I could love was to wait.

I waited for nothing.

6.

My fingers are making space
in her hair, ribbons
of space, rivers of air, the buds

upon buds of pussy willows
she brought me are bursting

with her, the shape
of her there.

RIVER

1.

As the plane flew in I followed
the river. Silver
ribbon, severed light,

I could take it in my hands.

2.

By the steps of Howard Hall where I
took piano lessons, a boy stood
by the door, his fly
unzipped, the thing
in his hand pink, like a toy
for a dog, he wagged
it like a finger.

3.

I have been leaving almost
everything out.

4.

Yesterday I slept in the bed
where my mother and father slept
when I was a child, knobs
at its corners, crescents cut
at the head and foot and dreamed
of a man—I had never wanted
anything quite like what I felt
that night, what I've left out
I left in his arms . . .

5.

Erase the board but the board
remains, returns,

even, gray or green, the eraser
eats the words.

6.

As the plane flew in I watched
the river, hearing the verb
to rive, what the river does
as it enters itself, barges trailing
their wakes like trains, to enter a space
that isn't my mother's steps
on the stairs she was waking
me out of a dream I was trying to end
that night a child I would not
let him see in the curve
of the river islands as if they were going
somewhere and now I am saying goodbye.

DOOR

1.

Sound me out

of this silent place   Oh listen

(if we could talk)

2.

Outside my office window
on the soccer field, seagulls
face a goal, they are a team

with no opponent

3.

Shell I think *pearl*
I think my hand

pearl pearl

4.

The space before the words
begin, or after the words, or between

the words, the opened

mouth between the words

5.

Not some window
through which to see the world
go by

Door, rather, opening
out and in

Nothing framed

6.

I love you, I
said, a small thing, a small sense
of something not
myself—

You

OPEN

1.

That yard half-blue with scylla,
no, *scilla:* little blue hats that opened
into stars, nothing more harmful
than stars, unless the sea
could ache like this—

2.

Mornings my body remembers
him. I am the mold, he
is the made.

Then I remember you.

3.

Last night I heard someone say,
Stalin was right to kill
those people, they were the bourgeoisie.

4.

Today by the couch where I said I need
you, the first time I said it
to anyone, is a vase of flowers, you
are away, they are tulips,
freesias, iris, white and blue.

5.

There is always someone it's right
to kill in the streets at night, it was not
a simple goodbye, he hurt me, I wanted to hurt
him back I am trying to say but I hurt
myself in those streets of dream.

6.

Open? my god I *am*
that yard but not
for anyone now but you and I
am waiting—that night I slept
in your arms all night, a river
between its banks—I am waiting for you.

ACKNOWLEDGMENTS

My thanks to the Bunting Institute of Radcliffe College, which gave me the space and time in and out of which the poems in "A Book of Days" were written.

My thanks as well to the following publications, in which these poems first appeared, some of them in different versions, with various titles: *Agni:* "A Book of Days" 12, 14, 16, 19, 26; *Antioch Review:* 17 (originally "Day"); *Crazyhorse:* 8; *Denver Quarterly:* 25, 27; *Field:* 10; *Five Fingers Review:* 5; *Harbor Review:* 21, 23; *Ironwood:* 2, 4; *The Journal:* 13, 18; *Louisville Review:* 22; *MSS:* 3; *Panoply:* 1; *Poet Lore:* "Women in American Literature: An Introduction"; *Prairie Schooner:* 9 (originally "Running"), "Door," "Open"; *Radcliffe Quarterly:* 30 (originally "Stripped"); *Seneca Review:* "Wind Chill," "River"; *Slant:* 7; *Snail's Pace Review:* "Hair"; *South Carolina Review:* 15; *Telescope:* 24; *Virginia Quarterly Review:* 6, 11; and *West Branch:* 20, 28, 29.

"Women in American Literature: An Introduction" is indebted to Nathaniel Hawthorne, Emily Dickinson, Henry James, James Fenimore Cooper, K.C. Frederick, and Elizabeth Cady Stanton, whose letters to Susan B. Anthony are quoted at the end of section 5.

ABOUT THE AUTHOR

Martha Collins' poems have appeared in many periodicals and anthologies, including *The Pushcart Prize X: Best of the Small Presses*. Her awards include a Bunting Fellowship, an Ingram Merrill Fellowship, an NEA Fellowship, and the Alice Fay Di Castagnola Award. Her first book of poems, *The Catastrophe of Rainbows,* was published by Cleveland State in 1985, and she has edited a collection of essays on Louise Bogan.

She teaches at the University of Massachusetts-Boston, where she established the creative writing program, and lives in Cambridge, Massachusetts.

THE PEREGRINE SMITH POETRY SERIES

Christopher Merrill, General Editor

Sequences, by Leslie Norris
Stopping by Home, by David Huddle
Daylight Savings, by Steven Bauer
The Ripening Light, by Lucile Adler
Chimera, by Carol Frost
Speaking in Tongues, by Maurya Simon
The Rebel's Silhouette, by Faiz Ahmed Faiz
(translated by Agha Shahid Ali)
The Arrangement of Space, by Martha Collins